The Number of Players: 2

The Object of the Game: To "catch" more fish than the other player.

The Playing Pieces: A pair of dice and 8 counters for each player, such as 8 paper clips for one player and 8 cereal pieces for the other.

The Play: Players take turns throwing the dice. On each turn the player chooses one number shown, doubles it, and then adds the number shown on the other die. If the total is the same as the number shown on one of the fish, then the player "catches" that fish by placing a counter on it. If a counter has already been placed on a fish with that total, then the player doubles the number shown on the second die, adds the number shown on the first die, and covers a fish with that total. If a counter has already been placed on a fish with the second total, then the player does not place a counter for that turn.

For example:
A player rolls a 3 and a 4.
The player can double the 3 and add 4 (3+3+4) to get a total of 10, or the player can double the 4 and add 3 (4+4+3) to get a total of 11.

The Winner: The first player to place 8 counters wins the game.

Math Concepts: Addition facts to 18. Doubling. Deductive reasoning.

I LOVE MATH

THE MYSTERY OF THE SUNKEN TREASURE

SEA MATH

TIME LIFE for Children
ALEXANDRIA, VIRGINIA

ALL ABOUT
I LOVE MATH

Look at page 6. There's something fishy going on there.

The *I Love Math* series shows children that math is all around them in everything they do. It can be found at the grocery store, at a soccer game, in the kitchen, at the zoo, even in their own bodies. As you collect this series, each book will fill in another piece of a child's world, showing how math is a natural part of everyday activities.

What Is Math?

Math is much more than manipulating numbers; the goal of math education today is to help children become problem solvers. This means teaching kids to observe the world around them by looking for patterns and relationships, estimating, measuring, comparing, and using reasoning skills. From an early age, children do this naturally. They divide up cookies to share with friends, recognize shapes in pizza, measure how tall they have grown, or match colors and patterns as they dress themselves. Young children love math. But when math only takes the form of abstract formulas on worksheets, children begin to dislike it. The *I Love Math* series is designed to keep math natural and appealing.

I found a new use for an old ice cream scoop. See pages 8 and 9.

How Do Children Learn Math?

Research has shown that children learn best by doing. Therefore, *I Love Math* is a hands-on, interactive learning experience. The math concepts are woven into stories in which entertaining characters invite children to help them solve math challenges. Activities reinforce the concepts, and special notes offer ways you can have more fun with this program.

SHELLY

We have worked closely with math educators to include in these books a full range of math skills. As the series progresses, repetition of these skills in different formats will help children master the basics of mathematical thinking.

What Will You Find in *Sea Math*?
In *Sea Math* you'll explore a coral reef and chart the number of creatures found there, analyze shell patterns at the beach, and use a tangram set to transform a brave boy into some fanciful forms. On a spectacular photographic sea voyage, you'll make up number stories about some fun-loving penguins and add and subtract with sea stars. You'll even learn a special technique for creating tessellated works of art.

When you're at the beach, try sorting shells by different attributes: size, shape, color, pattern. Then use your shells to create patterns on the sand. Check out the boats you see: How many masts and sails do they have? What shapes are the sails on each one? As you'll see, math is on the beach and in the sea, and we hope you'll say:

I LOVE MATH!

The Editors
Time-Life for Children

Turn to page 26 to see who gets in double trouble.

Table of Contents

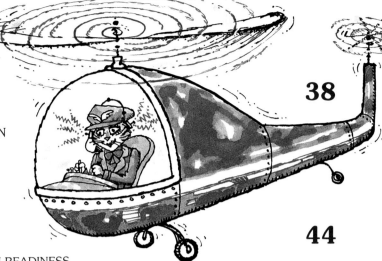

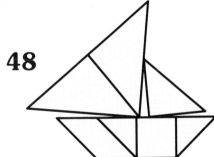

FISH-Y PARTY

Hey! Here is a group of 6 beautiful fish. All of the 6 fish in this group have tails. All of the 6 have fins.

But... only part of this group has stripes—5 of the 6 have stripes.

How many of this group of 6 fish have dots?

How many of this group of 6 fish do not have dots?

MATH FOCUS: FRACTIONS. By solving problems involving parts of a group, children explore the concept of fractions.

Have children put counters on the part of the group being described in each question.

What part of this group has some red?

And what part of this group has no red?

What part of this group has some white?
What part of this group has no white?

Uh-oh! The divers have scared 1 of the fish, and it swam away. Which fish do you think that was? Cover it, and then answer the divers' questions about the 5 brave fish who stayed.

MORE FUN. Take a small handful of multicolored jellybeans and make up questions about them. A possible question might be, "What part of this group is red?"

At the Seashore

How is my castle like Shelly's?

Which containers on these pages did Sandy use to build his sand castle?

Which containers did Shelly use to build her sand castle?

Which containers didn't Sandy use on his sand castle?

Which containers didn't Shelly use on her sand castle?

Who used more flags? How many more?

MATH FOCUS: GEOMETRY, PATTERNS, STATISTICS, SPATIAL SENSE, AND LOGICAL THINKING. Children solve different types of mathematical problems by analyzing sand castle shapes and the containers they were made from; investigating triangular and square shell patterns; and classifying shells found in Venn diagrams.

How is my castle different from Sandy's?

Which containers on these pages did Sandy use the most?
Of the containers Sandy used, which did he use the least?
Which container did Shelly use the most?
Of the containers Shelly used, which did she use the least?
Which container made a shape that looks like a cube?
Which container made a shape that looks like half a sphere?

MORE FUN. Using pennies, nickels, dimes, and quarters, make up your own progression pattern and challenge others to figure out what comes next.

Shelly arranged these shells in a pattern on the beach. Tell about the pattern you see. What would the next group to the right look like? How many shells would be in it?

Sandy made this pattern of shells. What would the next group to the right look like? How many shells would be in it?

Nine Silly Fishermen

Nine silly fishermen standing on the pier
In rows of three from there to here.

Look at the fishermen standing in the rows.
Where are the men with the sea stars on their toes?

Nine silly fishermen went fishing on Nantucket.
Which of the fishermen have fishes in a bucket?

Look at the fishermen across the top row.
What do they all have? Look closely. Do you know?

Start at the top and left, now look down diagonally.
They have one thing in common. What is it? Do you see?

Which of the fishermen have whiskers on their chins?
Point to the column that the bearded men are in.

Look at the men in the third column up and down.
Each fisherman has the same thing. Tell what you found.

Examine the fishermen across the middle row.
Each man has something special. What is it? Do you know?

Look at the men in the corners of the "square."
What is the same on each man standing there?

Look at the man who's exactly in the middle.
How is he different? Can you solve this fishy riddle?

MATH FOCUS: LOGICAL THINKING. Children use logical reasoning to classify groups of people by common attributes.

Tell children that rows go across, columns go up and down, and diagonals go in a slanting direction from corner to corner.

14

MORE FUN. Get three items that have one thing in common and six items that do not have that attribute, such as three buttons with holes and six buttons without holes. Arrange the three similar things in a row, a column, or diagonally. Then arrange the other items to form a 3 by 3 square. Make up a riddle about the three that are similar and challenge others to solve your riddle.

Tessellating Time

A famous Dutch artist, M.C. Escher, loved to create pictures with surprises in them.

The surprise in this picture is that the fish tessellate. That means that they fit together with no space between them. And all the fish are the same size and the same shape. Isn't that wonderful?

MATH FOCUS: GEOMETRY AND PATTERNS. By learning how to make a tessellation, children explore the beauty and fascination of mathematics. Among the surprises that children will find in these Escher pictures is his planning grid in the sea horse sketch.

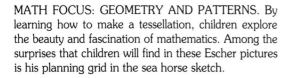

Tell children to tape their "nibble" piece directly opposite the spot from which it was cut, and not to use too much tape or the shape will not tessellate. Have children trace lightly around their shape so that they can redraw lines in areas that do not fit together.

What surprised you in these pictures? What did you see first? Then what did you see?

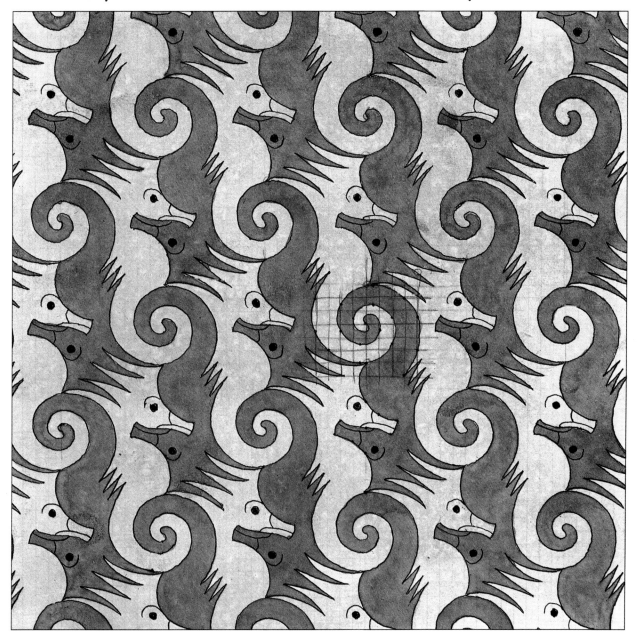

These sea horses tessellate, too. How did the artist color them? Why do you think he colored them that way? How did the artist decide to color the fish on page 16? Which color fish face left?

MORE FUN. Give your tessellation a name, sign and frame it, and then hang it up as your very own work of art.

Now you'll learn how to make a fish that tessellates. First we'll make the fish. Then we'll make a fishy tessellation!

Things you'll need:

1 Draw two squares next to each other.

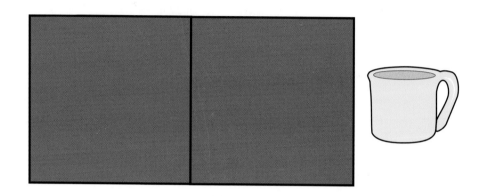

2 Trace around the bottom of a mug from corner to corner on the far right. Then do the same on the top right and bottom left.

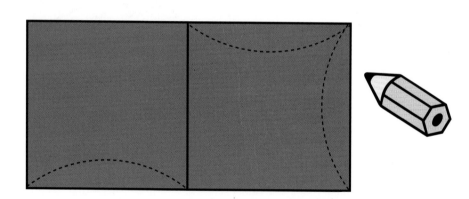

3 Cut out the piece from the far right. This is called a nibble.

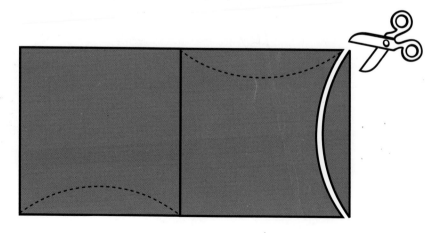

4 Take the nibble and slide it directly across to the opposite side. Tape it on.

5 Cut out the next nibble and slide it directly across to the opposite side. Tape it on.

6 Now cut out the last nibble and slide it to the opposite side. Tape it on.

7 Now give your fish a face.

19

Trace around your fish on a large piece of paper. Then trace around it until the page is filled. Make sure the fish fit together with no space between them.

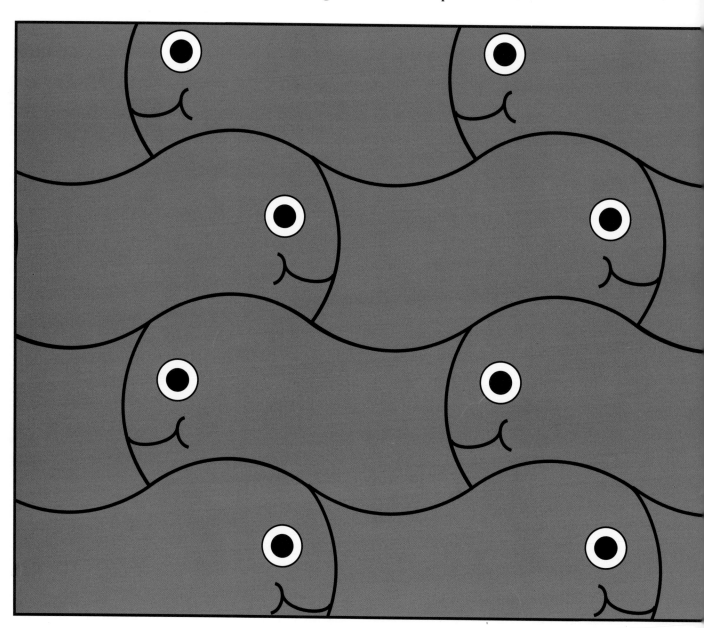

You can create more tessellations using this nibble and slide technique.

1. Start with a square.

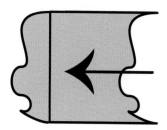

2. Cut a nibble from one side, slide it across to the opposite side, and tape it down.

Now give each fish an *eye* and a mouth. Color your fish. You've just made your own fishy tessellation!

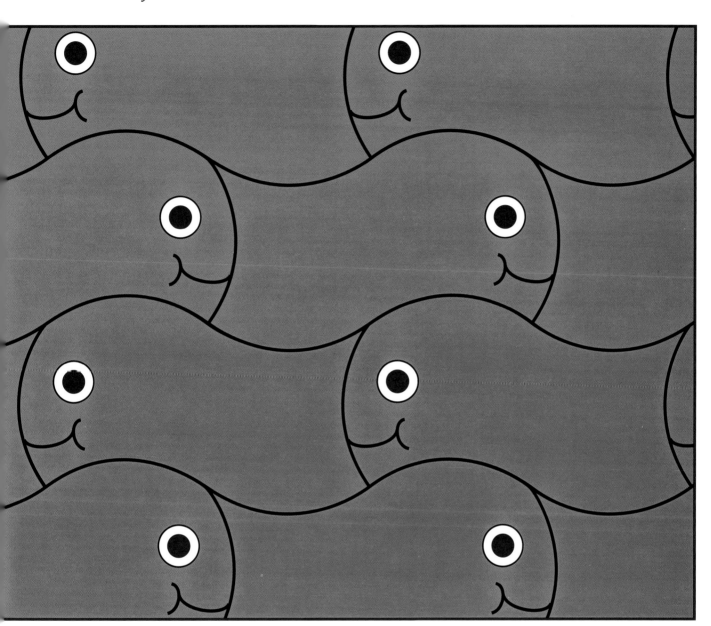

3. You can cut a nibble from another side, slide it, and tape it down.

4. What does your shape look like? Color it and give it a face if you want to. Then cover a piece of paper by tracing around it.

Charting the Waters

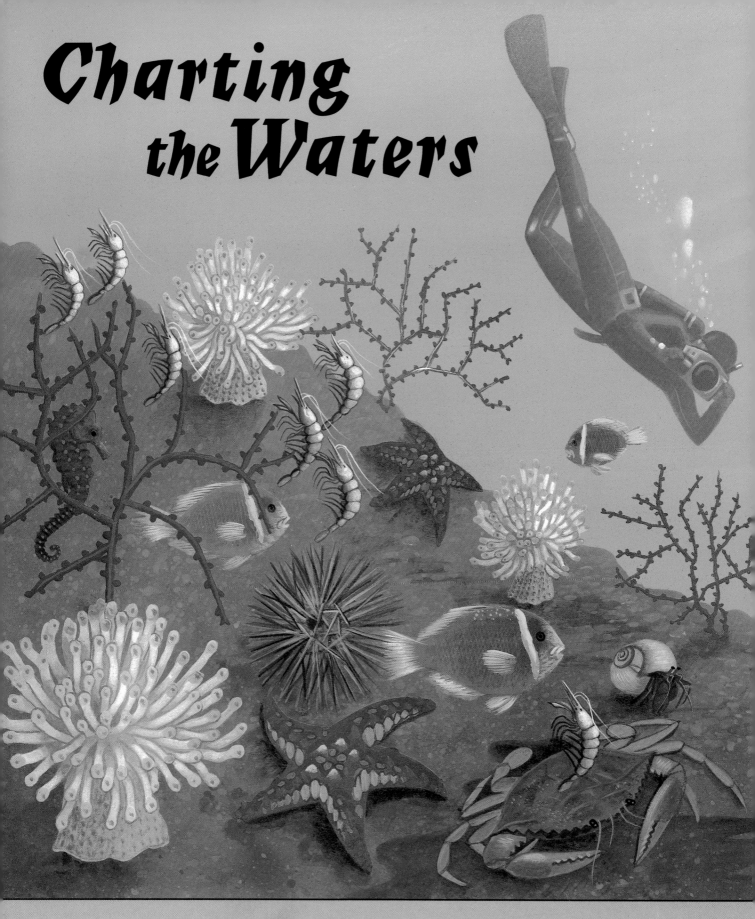

MATH FOCUS: STATISTICS. By using the data found on a pictograph and a bar graph to solve problems, children learn to analyze information.

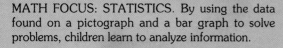

Have children evaluate each kind of graph and discuss the merits of each.

Wow! Look at all the different animals in the sea! How many different kinds can you find in this coral reef?

How many of each kind of animal are there? Count them and see. Then turn the page to find two different ways to record the number of each.

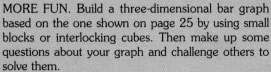

MORE FUN. Build a three-dimensional bar graph based on the one shown on page 25 by using small blocks or interlocking cubes. Then make up some questions about your graph and challenge others to solve them.

Animals in the Sea

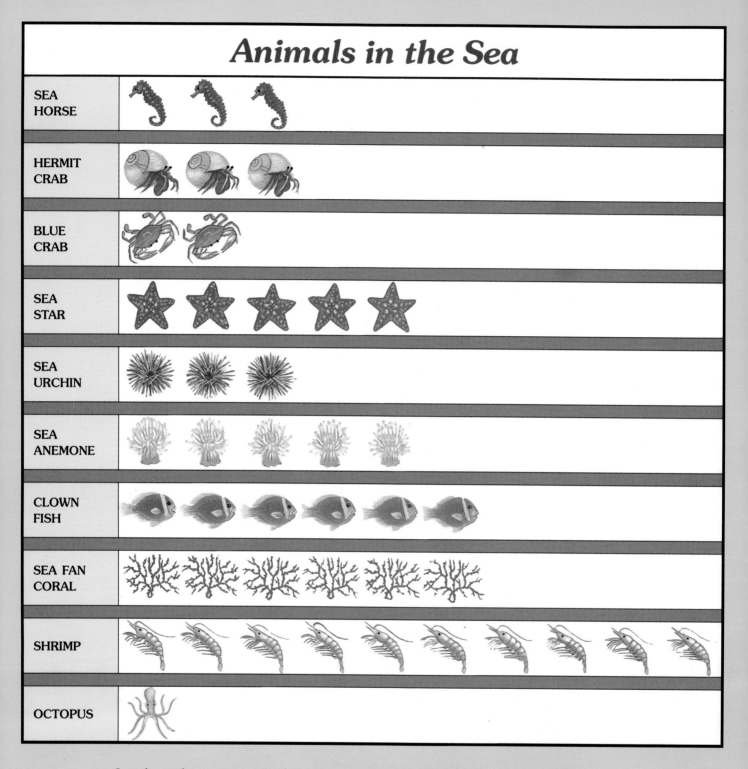

SEA HORSE	
SEA FAN CORAL	
HERMIT CRAB	
BLUE CRAB	
SEA STAR	
SEA URCHIN	
SEA ANEMONE	
CLOWN FISH	
SEA FAN CORAL	
SHRIMP	
OCTOPUS	

Look at these two graphs. They both chart the same information but in different ways. How are these graphs different? How are they the same?

As you answer the questions on page 25, tell which graph you used to find each answer and why you used that graph.

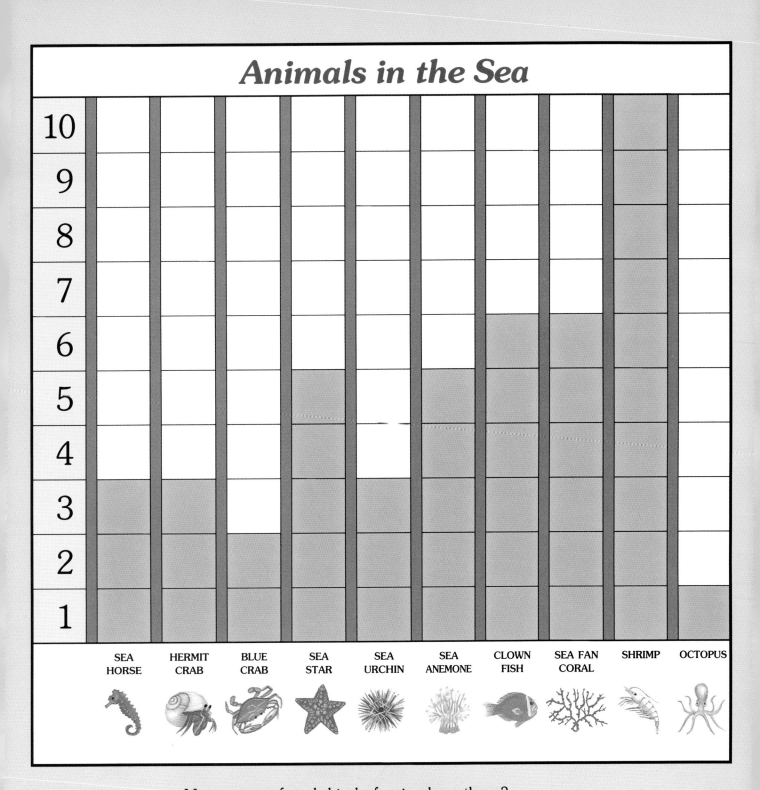

Animals in the Sea

| | SEA HORSE | HERMIT CRAB | BLUE CRAB | SEA STAR | SEA URCHIN | SEA ANEMONE | CLOWN FISH | SEA FAN CORAL | SHRIMP | OCTOPUS |

How many of each kind of animal are there?

Which animal are there the most of?

Which animal are there the fewest of?

How many more clown fish than sea urchins are there?

How many fewer sea fan corals than shrimp are there?

How many sea horses and sea stars are there altogether?

The Mystery of the Sunken Treasure

"Allo, Allo, Professor, this is Jackleen Mouseteau. I have a problem and I need you to come to the Florida Keys to help me. Is this possible?"

"But of course!" said Professor Guesser. "I will come at once!" She couldn't believe that Jackleen Mouseteau, the world-famous scuba diver, was calling her in on a case! She turned her helicopter and headed south.

MATH FOCUS: NUMBERS AND LOGICAL THINKING. Children explore the exponential growth that results when an amount is doubled, doubled again, and so on, over a fixed period of time.

Make a list of the number of coins Jackleen would get each day—Day 1: 1; Day 2: 2; Day 3: 4; Day 4: 8; Day 5: 16; Day 6: 32; Day 7: 64; Day 8: 128, and so on, to Day 14: 8192.

Professor Guesser arrived at Jackleen's dive shop in Key Largo.

"Mon cher professor," said Jackleen with a hug. "I am so happy to see you! I have such a big problem!"

"What can I do to help you?" asked Professor Guesser.

"Come sit down and I will tell you what has happened," said Jackleen.

MORE FUN. Use a calculator to find out the total number of coins Jackleen would get after a week.

"Many months ago, while I was photographing the giant squid, I discovered a 300-year-old pirate ship, a Spanish galleon sunk on a reef. In the hold was the pirate's treasure."

"How exciting!" gasped Professor Guesser.

"Oui! But I needed much equipment to salvage the treasure. This kind of venture is very expensive, no? I could not afford to dive the wreck alone. So I took a partner. His name is John La Feet. He provided the money for the salvage boat and the equipment, and I did all the diving."

"That seems like a fair arrangement," commented the professor.

"The first day, I brought up many gold coins, the next day many
more gold coins, and the day after even more, and the next day,
more still. It was fantastique! But now, Monsieur La Feet wants only
to pay me 100 of the gold coins that I salvaged. I do not think that
this is fair!" complained Jackleen.

"No, that doesn't seem fair," said Professor Guesser. "May I see
what you've recovered from the wreck?"

"But of course," said Jackleen.

Jackleen led Professor Guesser to a warehouse behind the dive shop. The professor's eyes nearly popped out of her head as the door opened to reveal the trunks full of gold coins that Jackleen had reclaimed from the pirate ship. "This is worth a great deal! How long did it take you to bring it up?" asked the professor.

"It took 2 weeks," said Jackleen proudly.

Professor Guesser counted the trunks. Then she estimated the total value of the treasure. The numbers were so huge, she had to use a calculator.

At last she said, "I have a plan to solve your problem. But, you must play along with me when we talk to Monsieur La Feet."

"I'll do whatever you say," promised Jackleen. "Let's go back to the shop. He's supposed to meet me there in five minutes."

Hmmm... Let me see. I estimate there are about 30,000 gold coins in these trunks.

The next day, Jackleen and Professor Guesser arrived at the warehouse just as John La Feet put the last coin down.

"Ooh la la," gasped Jackleen.

"You fooled me," barked Monsieur La Feet. "I never should have agreed to your ridiculous plan. Now I've lost everything. My entire fortune is gone!"

"Not your entire fortune," said Professor Guesser with a smile. "I estimate that you've paid Jacqueline about half of it."

"And that is fair, no?" laughed Jacqueline.

"That is fair, yes," said Professor Guesser.

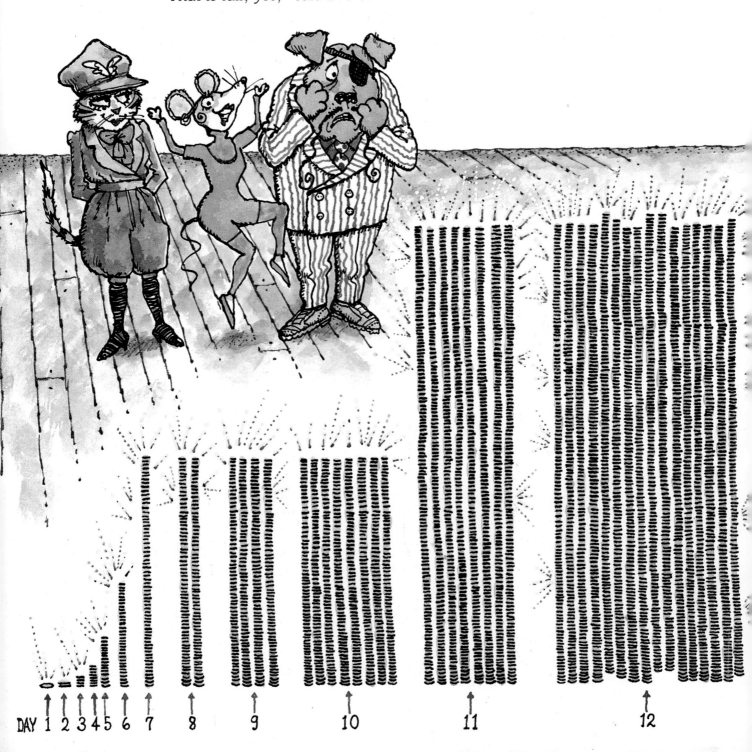

DAY 1 2 3 4 5 6 7 8 9 10 11 12

13   14

True Blue

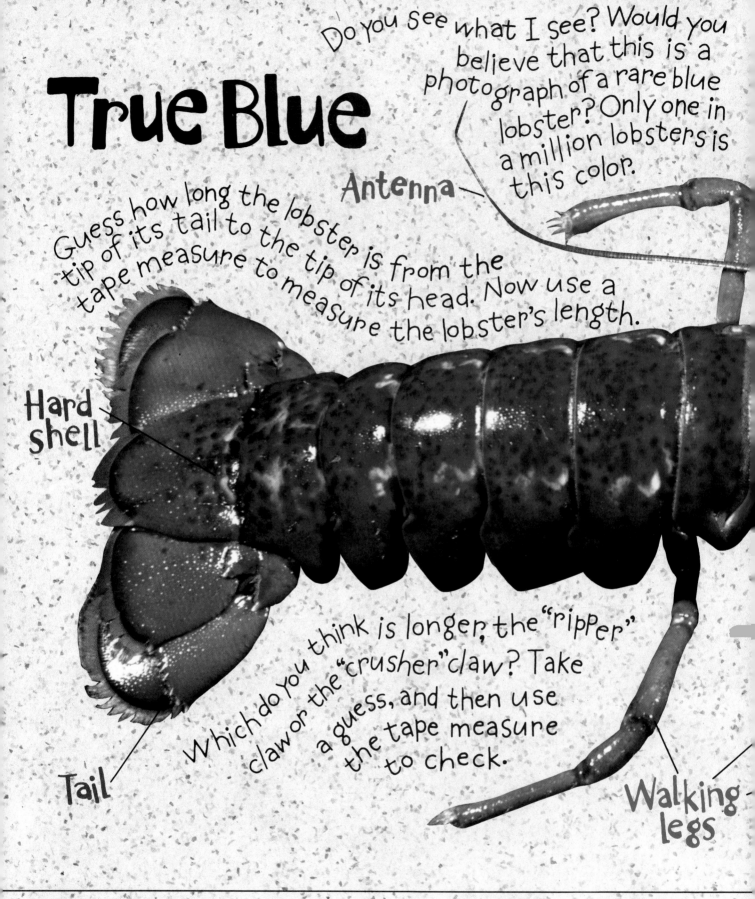

Do you see what I see? Would you believe that this is a photograph of a rare blue lobster? Only one in a million lobsters is this color.

Antenna

Guess how long the lobster is from the tip of its tail to the tip of its head. Now use a tape measure to measure the lobster's length.

Hard shell

Which do you think is longer, the "ripper" claw or the "crusher" claw? Take a guess, and then use the tape measure to check.

Tail

Walking legs

MATH FOCUS: ESTIMATION AND LENGTH—INCH. By estimating and then finding the lengths of things, children get direct measuring experience.

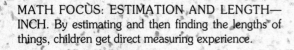

Tell children to measure the pincer part of each claw to find its length.

About how long do you think each antenna is? First guess, and then check with a tape measure.

"Crusher" claw

The lobster has the same number of walking legs on each side of its body. How many walking legs does it have altogether?

Head

Eye

Point to one walking leg. About how long is it? Guess. Then check by measuring.

"Ripper" claw

MORE FUN. Estimate and then measure the lengths of other things pictured in this book, for example the fish on pages 6 and 7.

NOW YOU SEA IT

Who's next? Make up a number story about this group of penguins.

A penguin swan dive? Can you tell a number story about these penguins?

ADELIE PENGUINS

MATH FOCUS: ESTIMATION, ADDITION, SUBTRACTION, ODD AND EVEN NUMBERS, AND SYMMETRY. By studying pictures of various sea creatures in their natural habitats, children explore several different areas of mathematics.

KING PENGUINS

About how many penguins are in this picture?
Are there more than 25? Are there fewer than 250?
Are there closer to 100 or closer to 200?

As children look for lines of symmetry on pages 42 and 43, tell them that some things in nature are "almost symmetrical" and that it is acceptable to have two halves that don't quite match.

MORE FUN. Read your penguin number story problems out loud and challenge others to determine which story problem goes with the picture on the top of page 38 and which goes with the picture on the bottom of page 38.

ROSE SEA STAR

Can you find two sea stars with a total of 15 arms?

Which sea stars have an even number of arms?

Which have an odd number?

BLUE SEA STAR

SUN SEA STAR

Add the number of arms that the blue sea star has to the number of arms that the six ray sea star has. Then find another sea star with that total.

40

Choose three sea stars. How many arms do they have altogether?

Which sea star is beginning to grow a new arm?

Six ray Sea Star

Sunflower Sea Star

Which two sea stars would you put together to get the greatest number of arms? How many arms would that be?

Purple Sea Star

The red string on this turtle divides the turtle into two matching sides, doesn't it? That means that the turtle is symmetrical. It has a line of symmetry.

All of these pictures have two matching sides. They are all symmetrical. Use string to show each picture's line of symmetry.

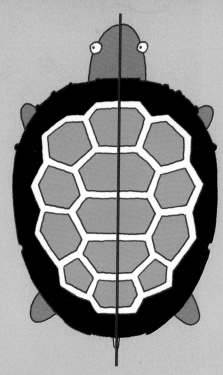

ROWING A SINGLE SCULL

AMERICAN FLAMINGO

42

PORCUPINEFISH

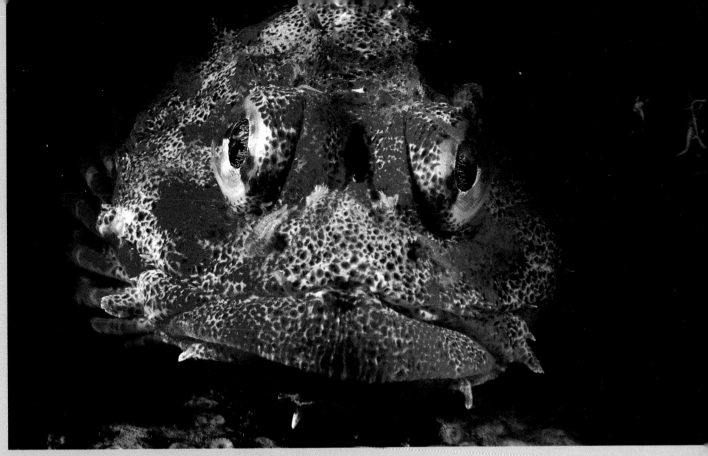

RED IRISH LORD

BUBBLE-EYE GOLDFISH

RED LAVA CRAB

Neil's Vacation

It takes Neil 8 minutes to swim from the beach to this island. How long does it take him to swim from the beach to the island and then back to the beach without stopping?

Half of the coconuts on this palm tree fell off and rolled away. How many coconuts used to be on this tree?

There are 5 huts on this beach. There are 2 people staying in each hut. How many people are staying in the huts? Where are they from?

MATH FOCUS: MULTIPLICATION READINESS, ADDITION, SUBTRACTION, AND TIME. By solving word problems, children learn to reason mathematically while applying several mathematical concepts and skills. They also decide when to add, subtract, or multiply.

Have available counters such as buttons or pennies. Encourage children to tell how they solved each problem.

There were a dozen birds in this group. How many are there now? How many flew away? Where did they go?

Neil spent 2 weeks at the beach. It was cloudy 3 of the days. It was sunny the rest of the time. How many days were sunny? What did Neil do on the cloudy days?

If 4 more fish show up to lie in the sun, how many will get inner tubes? How many won't? What will they do?

Neil got into the hammock 2 hours ago. It's now 3:30, What time did Neil get into the hammock? What is he thinking about?

This is Neil.

How many frogs can you find on this beach? How many frog legs do they have altogether?

MORE FUN. Make up three of your own problems about Neil's vacation and challenge others to solve them.

45

You are about to play with a toy that was invented 4000 years ago! That's a very old toy, and this is the legend of how it was invented.

TAN'S TILE

Once a man named Tan was taking his finest ceramic tile to the palace of the Emperor, when he tripped and broke the tile into seven pieces. Poor Tan was heartbroken as he frantically tried to put his precious tile back together again.

Alas, he could not fit the pieces back into the square shape that they once formed.

But to his amazement, other familiar figures, like the nearby pagoda and the cat that caught mice in his garden, could be made by arranging the broken pieces of tile. In fact, Tan discovered that he could make over 300 different pictures, or tangrams, from the seven simple shapes of his broken tile.

MATH FOCUS: GEOMETRY AND SPATIAL SENSE. By making their own tangram set, children get direct experience in investigating geometric shapes and their spatial relationships.

Help children trace and cut out the tangram pieces accurately.

THINGS YOU WILL NEED TO MAKE A TANGRAM SET:

- tracing paper
- pencil
- ruler
- heavy construction paper or tagboard
- scissors

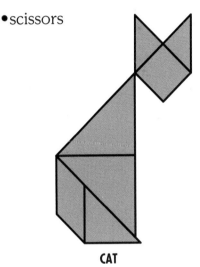

CAT

DIRECTIONS:

1. Place a sheet of tracing paper on the figure above.
2. Trace the black lines with your pencil and ruler.
3. Turn the tracing paper over and blacken the back of it with your pencil.
4. Place the tracing paper right-side-up on a sheet of construction paper.
5. Now retrace the lines on the tracing paper to make an imprint on the construction paper.
6. Cut the construction paper along the lines.

Experiment with these seven puzzle pieces to see if you can make a picture. Then read *The Story of Chu* on the following pages. Try to make the tangram pictures that are found in the story. Good luck!

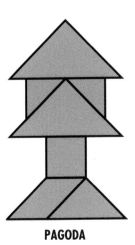

PAGODA

MORE FUN. Use three tangram pieces to make a square; then use four pieces to make a square. Now try to make a triangle with three pieces.

THE STORY OF

Very long ago, by the shore of the China Sea, there lived a young boy named Chu. One morning, Chu's mother sent him off to the market with a small handful of coins to buy a sack of rice.

MATH FOCUS: GEOMETRY AND SPATIAL SENSE. By using their own tangram set to copy tangram pictures, children get direct experience in investigating geometric shapes and their spatial relationships.

48

Have children make each tangram picture as the story progresses.

On his way, one of the Emperor's guards stopped Chu. "Where are you going?" bellowed the guard.

"To market," replied Chu.

"Give me some of your money for the Emperor," said the guard.

"I can not," said Chu. "This money is for rice that will feed my family." And he ran away.

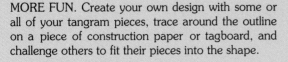

MORE FUN. Create your own design with some or all of your tangram pieces, trace around the outline on a piece of construction paper or tagboard, and challenge others to fit their pieces into the shape.

The Emperor's guard chased Chu as he fled into the cold churning ocean.

"I have him now," thought the guard. But low and behold, Chu became a fish.

The guard rubbed his eyes in disbelief as Chu swam away. "I'll catch him yet!" he vowed. The guard got a fishing rod and cast his line into the water.

But just as the Emperor's guard was about to hook him on the line, Chu turned into a boat and sailed away.

The Emperor's guard called for the Emperor's oarsmen so they could follow Chu out to sea. The oarsmen rowed and rowed closer and closer to Chu. The guard leaned out of the boat toward Chu.

Just as the Emperor's guard was about to seize Chu, Chu changed into a seagull and flew away. The guard fell into the cold waters of the China Sea and came up sputtering and coughing.

"Follow that gull!" ordered the Emperor's guard.

The oarsmen pulled the Emperor's guard out of the water and rowed back to shore as fast as they could.

Chu flew down to the beach and called out to the Emperor's guard. "Will you give up and let me have my money so my family can eat?"

"Never," said the guard. And he began to chase Chu again.

This time, Chu landed on the beach and changed himself into a crab. He began to cover himself with sand. In no time at all Chu was completely hidden under the sand.

The Emperor's guard was furious. He dove to the ground and thrust his arm deep into the sand where he had last seen Chu.

"I have you now," he laughed.

"I warn you. Let me go," said Chu. "Let me go!"

"Never!" shouted the guard.

53

His enormous hand pulled Chu from the hole. But Chu was no longer a crab. He was a fireworks rocket.

The Emperor's guard jumped back in fear. Up, up, up into the air sailed Chu. Then the fireworks began. The sky was filled with a rainbow of sparkling lights.

The Emperor came out to his balcony to watch the show. When the fireworks stopped, the Emperor turned around and there stood Chu.

Who are you?" asked the startled Emperor.

"I am Chu," replied the boy.

"Ah, Chu!" said the Emperor.

Chu gave him a handkerchief and said, "I know you are wise and honest. But one of your guards tried to take the money that my mother gave me to buy rice to feed our family."

"Tell me who it is, and that man will be punished," said the outraged Emperor.

"Assemble your guards. The guilty man will let the cat out of the bag," said Chu as he disappeared into the night.

The following morning, the Emperor lined up all of his guards within the palace walls. He remembered the clue that Chu had given him the night before, and he said,

"There is the guilty man!"

Which of the Emperor's guards is the one that chased Chu?

Sailing, Sailing

FOUR-MASTED BARK
TALLEST MAST   about 150 feet
DRAFT   about 20 feet

BRIG
TALLEST MAST   about 90 feet
DRAFT   about 10 feet

Masts are tall poles that hold the sails on sailboats.

Which boat has the tallest mast? Which one has the shortest?

Which boat has the greatest number of masts? Which has the fewest? Which boat has twice as many masts as the brig?

MATH FOCUS: LENGTH/HEIGHT/DEPTH AND LARGER NUMBERS. Children solve measurement problems by comparing the data for four different boats.

Help children use the graph on the bottom of page 57. Discuss the relationship of ship size and draft.

SLOOP

TALLEST MAST	about 60 feet
DRAFT	about 5 feet

FULL-RIGGED SHIP

TALLEST MAST	about 120 feet
DRAFT	about 15 feet

The draft is how deep the water must be for the boat to float.

Which boat needs the least water depth?
Which boat needs the most?
The full-rigged ship has a draft of 15 feet.
Could it sail in water that is 10 feet deep?
Which two boats could sail in water that is 10 feet deep?
Which boats could sail in water that is 15 feet deep?

MORE FUN. Where would you place a sailboard and an ocean liner on the draft graph? Estimate about how much draft each boat would need to stay afloat.

How do puffins GRAPH their muffins?

Once on an island
Sat three hungry puffins
Who dined every day
On blueberry muffins.

"I wonder how many
Of these we devour?"
Thought Sam one bright morning
While taking a shower.
"We should keep track,
And graph all our muffins."

He told his idea
To the other two puffins.

MATH FOCUS: STATISTICS AND MULTIPLICATION
READINESS. Children solve problems by using data
from pictographs showing 1 to 1 correspondence, 5
to 1 correspondence, and 10 to 1 correspondence.

Point out each muffin key on page 61. Have children
count by ones to find the number of muffins Sam ate,
by fives to find the number of muffins Zack ate, and
by tens to find the number of muffins Jane ate.

How did Sam make his graph?
Here is a clue.
For each muffin he ate,
A muffin he drew!
At the end of a week
He'd eaten this many.
How much were they worth
If they each cost a penny?

When Zack ate his muffins,
His graphing was great!
One muffin he drew
For each five that he ate.
Here is his graph
At the end of one week.
How many muffins
Had passed through his beak?

This was Jane's rule:
She ate muffins and then
Drew just one muffin
When she'd eaten ten.
This was her graph
After she'd eaten plenty.
How many, you ask?
It must have been . . .

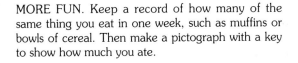MORE FUN. Keep a record of how many of the
same thing you eat in one week, such as muffins or
bowls of cereal. Then make a pictograph with a key
to show how much you ate.

59

Then they decided
To compare all three graphs,
And Sam, Zack, and Jane Puffin
Started to laugh.

Sam said with pride,
"I am not one to boast.
Jane and Zack ate 2 muffins each.
I ate the most."

"I ate more than 2 muffins,"
Jane said to Sam.
"I had 20 muffins
With butter and jam."

Sam said, "Look at your graphs.
You don't know how to count.
There are only 2 muffins
To show your amount."

Then Zack said to both of them,
"Look, don't you see?
Each of our muffin graphs
Is missing a key."

So each puffin scribbled
A key at the top.
The problem was solved,
And the argument stopped.

The key on each graph
Will allow you to find
The muffins each ate
Of the blueberry kind.

If Zack's graph showed 3 muffins, how many muffins would he have eaten?

If Jane's graph showed 5 muffins, how many muffins would she have eaten?

MATH FOCUS: LOGICAL THINKING AND ADDITION. By using a calculator to solve a number riddle, children practice adding while using the strategy of guess and test to find the correct answer.

Tell children to use the number line at the bottom of these pages to help them.

Now I pick 14.

Yes! 5 and 6 are neighboring numbers, and they add up to 11.

Thank you. I'm glad I have my calculator to help me. Hmmm....

Remember that you can use more than two neighboring numbers.

Did you find any neighboring numbers that add up to 14?

Yes, I did.
2 + 3 + 4 + 5 = 14

Pick another number from 1 to 20. See if you can make it by adding neighboring numbers. Be careful! There are 5 numbers between 1 and 20 that can't be made by adding neighboring numbers!

11 12 13 14 15 16 17 18 19 20

MORE FUN. Use a calculator to make these numbers from neighboring numbers: 29; 33; 57.

TIME-LIFE for CHILDREN®

Assistant Managing Editor: Patricia Daniels
Editorial Directors: Jean Burke Crawford, Allan Fallow,
    Karin Kinney, Sara Mark
Marketing: Margaret Mooney
Financial Analyst: Tim Brown
Publishing Assistant: Marike van der Veen
Production Manager: Marlene Zack
Production: Celia Beattie
Supervisor of Quality Control: James King
Assistant Supervisor of Quality Control:
    Miriam Newton

Produced by Kirchoff/Wohlberg, Inc.
866 United Nations Plaza
New York, New York 10017

Series Director: Mary Jane Martin
Creative Director: Morris A. Kirchoff
Mathematics Director: Jo Dennis
Designer: Jessica A. Kirchoff
Assistant Designers: Daniel Moreton, Judith Schwartz
Contributing Writer: Anne M. Miranda
Managing Editor: Nancy Pernick
Editors: Susan M. Darwin, David McCoy

Cover Illustration: Don Madden

Illustration Credits: Liz Callen, pp. 44–45; Oki Han, pp.
46–55; Roberta Holmes, pp. 14–15, 58–61; Tom Leonard,
pp. 22–25, 57; Don Madden, pp. 26–35, back end papers;
Daniel Moreton, front end papers, pp. 62–63; Diane Paterson,
pp. 8–13; Joe Veno, pp. 6–7.

Page 16, © 1953 M.C. Escher Foundation–Baarn–Holland–
Cordon Art B.V.; page 17, © 1952 M.C. Escher Foundation–
Baarn–Holland–Cordon Art B.V.

First printing. Printed in U.S.A.
Published simultaneously in Canada.

Time Life Inc. is a wholly owned subsidiary of THE TIME INC.
BOOK COMPANY

Time-Life is a trademark of Time Warner Inc. U.S.A.

For subscription information, call 1-800-621-7026.
School and library distribution by Time-Life Education
P.O. Box 85026, Richmond, VA 23285-5026

CONSULTANTS

Mary Jane Martin spent 17 years working in elementary
school classrooms as a teacher and reading consultant; for
seven of those years she was a first-grade teacher. The
second half of her career has been devoted to publishing.
During this time she has helped create and produce a wide
variety of innovative elementary programs, including two
mathematics textbook series.

Jo Dennis has worked as a teacher and math consultant in
England, Australia, and the United States for more than 20
years. Most recently, she has helped develop and write several
mathematics textbooks for kindergarten, first grade, and
second grade.

Photography Credits: Pages 8–13, Justin Kirchoff; 41(b),
Fred Bavendam, Peter Arnold, Inc.; 42(cl), Karl Weatherly,
Tony Stone Images; 56(br), Mathew Pundt; 57(tr), Guido
Alberto Rossi, The Image Bank; ALLSTOCK: 38(t), 39,
42(br), Art Wolfe; 38(b), Gregory G. Dimijian; 42(bl), Norbert
Wu; 43(t), F. Stuart Westmorland; ANIMALS ANIMALS:
40(bl), W. Gregory Brown; 41(tr), Adrienne T. Gibson;
43(bl), Patti Murray; 43(br), Max Gibbs, Oxford Scientific
Films; BRUCE COLEMAN, INC.: 40(t), Steve Solum; 40(cr),
41(cl), R. Mariscal; PHOTO RESEARCHERS: 6(tl),
Pecolatto, Jacana; 6(cr), Toni Angermayer; 6(bl), A.W.
Ambler; 7(tl), 7(bl), Fred McConnaughey; 7(cr), David Hall;
36–37, P.W. Grace; 56(t), Richard Ellis; 57(tl), Fritz Henle.

Sand castles on pages 8 and 9 constructed by Jennifer McCandlish.

Library of Congress Cataloging-in-Publication Data
The mystery of the sunken treasure : sea math.
        p.   cm. — (I love math)
    ISBN 0-8094-9994-0
    1. Mathematics—Juvenile literature. 2. Marine
fauna—Juvenile literature. [1. Mathematics. 2. Marine
animals.] I. Time-Life for Children (Firm) II. Series.
QA40.5.M96   1993
511'.6—dc20   93-35986
                                                    CIP
                                                    AC